FRENCH POS

T&J

Published by TAJ Books International LLC 2014
5501 Kincross Lane
Charlotte, North Carolina, USA
28277

www.tajbooks.com
www.tajminibooks.com

ISBN 978-1-84406-336-9
978-1-62732-014-6 Paperback

Printed in China

1 2 3 4 5 18 17 16 15 14

FRENCH POSTERS

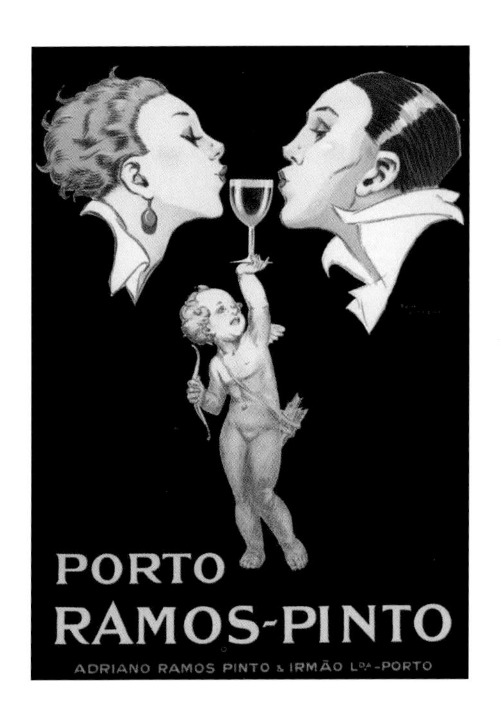

ISABELLA ALSTON & KATHRYN DIXON

INTRODUCTION

The poster has been around for hundreds of years, serving first and foremost as a means of communication. The simplest definition of a poster is any form of paper with a printed design or text that is created to be hung on a vertical surface. The poster's genesis was purely a textual form, most often used for displaying government decrees. One of the earliest, more developed forms of poster was a means of advertisement, such as for one of Shakespeare's plays. Eventually, posters came to be used as a way to spread propaganda, especially during wartime. Another common use of posters is as a cheap and efficient way to mass-produce popular artworks for the general public's consumption.

As the printing process became more modernized and streamlined, posters began to include images in addition to text. With the invention of color printing, the poster slowly evolved until its focus was primarily the visual image rather than the text, because an image could relay the desired message more quickly. The purpose of the poster image was to catch the eye of the passerby so that he or she would look more closely at the text for more detailed information.

The tremendous success of the poster can be attributed to one man, Alois Senefelder, and his groundbreaking invention, lithography. Alois Senefelder (1771 to 1834) was a German playwright and actor. He soon discovered that he preferred writing plays more than performing them. But when he began to fall into debt to his local printer, he began to experiment with new, non-commercial forms of printing.

Senefelder found that he could apply chemicals to a block of fine-grained stone, such as limestone (Germany is renowned for its Solnhofen limestone, which is especially fine-grained and thus ideal for retaining fine details), and the chemicals would literally "etch" the image or text he had created onto the stone. After wetting the etched stone, he could roll grease-based ink over it. The etched areas of the stone (i.e., the desired image) retained the ink, while the un-etched, or negative, areas repelled it. Paper could then be laid down on the inked limestone block, put through a press, and the inked image would be transferred to the paper.

The limestone block could be re-used countless times to print the image. When the printer wanted to change the image, all he needed to do was to sand down the etched layer and re-start the process on the limestone block. Thus, Senefelder discovered the first planographic printing process (i.e., printing from a flat surface as opposed to a raised or incised surface) that was put to commercial use. Lithography not only allowed easy mass-production of posters for commercial reasons,

The American dancer Loïe Fuller performing her infamous Serpentine Dance (above) and an artistic rendering of the same by Jean de Paleologu (1855-1942) to promote Fuller's appearance at the Folies Bergère nightclub in Paris.

but also helped turn the poster into an accepted and popular form of art. Lithography is taught in art schools today as its own art form. Some of the most well-known artists to utilize the poster as an art form are Henri Toulouse-Lautrec and Alphonse Mucha.

Henri Raymond de Toulouse-Lautrec-Monfa (1864 to 1901), more often referred to simply as Toulouse-Lautrec, was an artist primarily based in Paris during the late 19th century. He was born to a French aristocratic family and spent a good part of his childhood drawing and sketching. Throughout his life he was plagued by an undefined congenital health problem, which many have attributed to a family history of inbreeding. From a young age, he suffered from brittle bones that never fully healed after they broke, and as he aged, these malformed bones inhibited his natural growth and resulted in his unusually short stature. Although his torso was a normal adult size, his legs never grew longer than their length when he was 13 years old.

Toulouse-Lautrec's physical handicaps effectively pushed him to pursue artistic studies because he was unable to participate in most other activities. Thanks to his family's aristocratic influence, he was able to study under the guidance of the prominent French painter Léon Bonnat. Toulouse-Lautrec eventually found his niche in Montmarte, the bustling Bohemian neighborhood in Paris. Writers, artists, and philosophers from every walk of life and from all corners of the world co-mingled there in the mid- to late-19th century, influencing each other's creative process and inspiring new, modern, freer forms of expression.

Some of Toulouse-Lautrec's first subjects were the prostitutes of Montmarte, which would lead to his later, very famous paintings and posters of Paris' dance hall girls. His early style is somewhat reminiscent of the Dutch artist Vincent van Gogh, with whom he was acquainted. As the years passed, Toulouse-Lautrec's images became more abstract representations of the women of Montmarte.

Moulin Rouge, 1900

Toulouse-Lautrec's first official contract for creating poster art was for Moulin Rouge, a cabaret in Pigalle near Montmarte that was topped with a red windmill. Toulouse-Lautrec's attention-grabbing posters that depicted the cabaret's dancing girls doing the wildly suggestive cancan, and especially of the cabaret's star performer Jane Avril, made Moulin Rouge one of the most well-known cabarets in all of history.

Alphonse Mucha (1860 to 1939) is another artist well known for his artwork that graced countless posters at the turn of the 20th century. Mucha was born in what is now the Czech Republic. Since a young child, Mucha had exhibited artistic talent. After graduating from high school, he collaborated with his brother and a friend to form a decorative painting business, primarily murals for public buildings. He also worked for a few years in Vienna, Austria, for a theatrical design company. Mucha continued to freelance and was soon hired by Count Karl Khuen who requested that Mucha decorate his castle with murals. Mucha's work pleased the count so much that he offered to pay for him to attend the Munich Academy of Fine Arts so that he could receive formal training.

After graduating from the academy, Mucha moved to Paris. To support himself, he worked for a printing company. He was luckily in the right place at the right time one day in 1894, when he was the only artist in the office and was tasked with designing a poster for Sarah Bernhardt, the most famous actress in all of Europe. Mucha's poster depicts an image of Bernhardt in the role of Gismonda, her name encircling and framing her face. The poster was produced using lithography, as were most during this period, and attracted much attention due to its beauty and uniqueness. Bernhardt was so impressed by Mucha's work and the success his work brought her that she offered him a long-term contract. Mucha's posters of Bernhardt led to his fame, and his unique artistic style is what initially began the Art Nouveau movement. In addition to the Bernhardt posters, Mucha began to receive a flood of other commissions, ranging from magazine ads to menus, postcards, and calendars.

Another Parisian artist, Jules Chéret (1836 to 1932), developed a new and improved method of lithography that could accept significantly more color than the old method. Advertisers preferred the new method because the bright colors were better able to catch the public's eye. Suddenly, the streets of Paris were ablaze with color as buildings and billboards became plastered with vibrant images of poster art.

Chéret had begun his career as an apprentice to a lithography company in Paris and moved to London for more training. When he returned to Paris he designed numerous advertising posters for theaters and cabarets, in particular the Folies Bergère. His favorite subjects were women. These women, rendered with some degree of modesty, were so popular that they were readily recognized throughout the city and the country as "the Chérettes."

Due to Sarah Bernhardt's most successful collaboration with the artist Alphonse Mucha, lesser known actors and actresses began to hire their own personal poster artist, causing demand to steadily increase for artists who were willing and able to produce posters. Taking heed of the popularity of posters, Chéret introduced the *Maîtres de l'Affiche* series in 1895. The collection helped to define the poster as art, not only as advertising. The series included 256 lithographic plates of the original work of 97 artists. Chéret sent each subscriber a set of four prints on a monthly basis over a subscription period of five years. These posters also suggested the value of sexuality in selling products, since the majority of the artists chose to portray women in their posters.

Adolphe Mouron (1901 to 1968), more simply known as Cassandre, is credited with innovative graphic-design solutions in advertising, which he successfully employed in the years before World War II. The enormous, hulking prow of the *Normandie* trans-Atlantic ocean liner is one of the most famous and iconic in the history of poster design; it was created by Cassandre. Cassandre was born in Ukraine, but moved to Paris in the 1920s, thriving in the city's creative and artistic environment. After studying at the Ecole des Beaux-Arts and the Académie Julian, and influenced by Cubist and Surrealist imagery, he began to incorporate that imagery into his designs in poster making. By the mid-1930s, he was being commissioned to design magazine covers by such periodicals as *Harper's Bazaar*. He was also an innovator in designing typeface. Today, he is best known for his travel posters.

Other lesser-known French poster artists were Julien Lacaze (1886 to 1971) Léo Lelée (1872 to 1947), Guillaume Georges Roger (1867 to 1974), and René Vincent (1879 to 1936). Roger specialized in travel posters and Vincent in automobiles.

Of course, the poster as art form was not the sole territory of French artists–artists of many other nationalities contributed to the wide variety of poster images. One of Italy's leading poster artists was Marcello Dudovich (1878 to 1962) who is known for his vibrantly colored, dramatic ads on black backgrounds, similar to the style of Leonetto Cappiello (1875 to 1942), an Italian who lived and worked in France.

J. & W. Beggarstaff was the pseudonym created by two British artists, William Nicholson and James Pryde, for their artistic collaboration on graphic design and posters from 1894 to 1899. When Nicholson was in art school, he met his future wife, with whom he eloped shortly thereafter. Once the two had found a home and settled in, his wife's brother, Pryde, came to visit. An actor acquaintance, Edward Gordon Craig, was to tour in Hamlet in the summer of 1894. He asked Pryde and Nicholson to design a promotional poster for the play.

This inauspicious encounter marked the beginning of the two artists' collaboration.

The prototype for the first poster began as a partial collage in which Craig's clothing and hair was cut from black paper. His figure was then stenciled onto brown wrapping paper with hand-drawn details added later. The original poster is not believed to have survived. The pair went on to collaborate on numerous other posters, but their best-known work remains the Hamlet poster.

Théophile Alexandre Steinlen (1859 to 1923) was a Swiss-born Art Nouveau painter and printmaker. He was born in Lausanne where he attended university. After graduating, he found a job as an apprentice designer in a textile mill in eastern France. On the side, he painted. One day the painter Francois Bocion encouraged the young Steinlen and his wife to relocate to Montmartre in Paris. Bocion knew in this invigorating environment Steinlen's talent could truly flourish. He could make contacts and surround himself with other artists and creative spirits.

In Paris, Steinlen met Adolphe Willette, another painter, who brought Steinlen to the Le Chat Noir cabaret. Steinlen meet the nightclub's owner, who eventually commissioned him to create poster art for the club. Steinlen's work was shown at Paris' Les Salon des Indépendants, indicating his success in the Parisian art world. His work focused on life in Montmartre, both the good and the bad sides of the community. He later attempted a few sculptures, primarily of cats of which he was quite fond.

Whereas posters were extremely popular in Europe, America did not initially share the same fondness for the art form. Alphonse Mucha discovered this when, in later years after already achieving success in Europe, he moved to New York. Finding work for himself as a poster artist was rather difficult; Americans, unlike the Europeans (especially the Parisians), did not revere the image on the poster as the most important element of the advertiser's message. Eventually, Americans' perception of the poster changed when posters began to be used to sell the traveling circus, for which bright and colorful poster images mirrored the reality of the performers in the circus ring. Nevertheless, circus posters—viewed as more utilitarian and less as artwork—have never been considered of the same caliber as the European posters of the era.

Most vintage French posters can be described as being of the Art Nouveau style or the Art Deco style. An easy way to tell the two styles apart is that Art Nouveau is flowery and decorative, whereas Art Deco is streamlined and sleek. Both the Art Nouveau and Art Deco movements emerged as reactions to major world events: the Industrial Revolution and World War I, respectively. The Art Nouveau period stretched from roughly 1880, the dawn of the Indusrial Revolution, until just before World War I. The Industrial Revolution was welcomed by certain artists who embraced the possibilities of new materials, such as cast iron, which were available to artists with the progress in technology. Yet other artists deplored the shoddiness of mass-produced, machine-made goods and chose to elevate the decorative arts by applying the highest standards of craftsmanship and design to mundane objects. Both viewpoints informed the Art Nouveau style.

Art Nouveau designers believed that all the arts (buildings, furniture, textiles, clothes, and jewelry) should work in harmony to create a "total work of art." Art Nouveau features naturalistic but stylized forms, often combined with geometric shapes, particularly arcs and semicircles. The movement introduced natural forms such as insects, weeds, and even mythical faeries, represented, for example, in Lalique jewelry and Tiffany lamps.

Art Deco emerged after World War I and, following the deprivations of the war years, focused on renewed opulence and extravagance that would come to define the Jazz Age and the Art Deco aesthetic. The movement, from the 1920s until roughly the start of World War II, took its name from France's 1925 Exposition Internationale des Arts Décoratifs et Industriels Modernes (a poster advertising the exposition is on the facing page), which featured art and objects characterized by streamlined, strongly geometric shapes.

During the First and Second World Wars, posters were a popular way to promote nationalist propaganda and other information as well as to help urge young men to enlist and protect their homeland. These posters displayed images and phrases, which spoke to the individual's patriotism, and bombarded the general public with a striking message designed to elicit a strong emotional response. Some of the best known are not French at all, but were

created for U.S. and U.K. audiences. In the U.S., the crusty old character of Uncle Sam ("I want you!"), created by J.M. Flagg, was introduced in a World War I poster campaign.

Color woodblock poster for the Paris 1925 Exhibition, by Robert Bonfils (1886 to 1972) for Imprimerie Vaugirard, Paris, France (1925), Victoria and Albert Musuem, London

In World War II, J. Howard Miller's "Rosie the Riveter" poster quickly became an iconic American image, created to help encourage women to contribute to the war effort by working in the munitions factories. The poster pictures a woman in factory clothes flexing her arm with the phrase "We Can Do It!" scrawled boldly across the top of the poster.

During World War II, the U.K. produced a poster (but surprisingly never distributed it) that read "Keep Calm and Carry On" in an effort to reassure the British public who found themselves daily victims of the terrors of war with Nazi Germany.

In recent years, all three of these well-known posters have experienced renewed popularity, albeit in rather dramatically revamped interpretations designed to appeal to modern society. Surely, the combination of graphic and advertising savvy inherent in these posters, which have retained their applicability and attention-getting power over multiple generations, marks them as truly memorable advertising and informational campaigns; good design proven to stand the test of time.

Posters were (and still are) used extensively to advertise the cinema, just as they were used in pre-cinema days to promote stage actors and plays. The movie poster was easily pasted on buildings, lamp posts, and outside theatres, providing a snapshot preview of what the movie was all about. These cinematic poster images were designed to stimulate intrigue and excitement about the movie. Today, some older movie posters are quite valuable. Numerous avid collectors are in the marketplace.

The "Mona Lisa" of movie posters is the poster for Fritz Lang's movie *Metropolis* (1925). It sold in 2005 for $690,000 before turning up again in a bankruptcy auction in 2012 when it sold along with several other rare movie posters as a group for $1.2 million. The original 1931 six-sheet poster for *Frankenstein* may be the most valuable movie poster out there; only one copy is known to exist and it has never been sold.

The travel poster is yet another form of the genre. Most originated in the 1920s and 1930s, between the two World Wars when travel and leisure were easily accessible and once again possible for many. Most of these posters depicted top destinations around the world, especially resort locales. They consist of beautifully drawn images of the location, often showing vacationers enjoying the pleasures of the resort, and usually include the name of the location in bold lettering on the bottom portion of the frame.

Travel posters were not only relegated to destinations, but were also used to advertise modes of transportation to these destinations. Posters, such as those by Cassandre, depicting cruise ships and steamers were the first wave of transport posters, followed later by posters advertising travel by train. Eventually, with the advent of the airplane, posters promoted the airlines as well.

Today, the majority of posters are no longer produced using the lithographic method. Technology has allowed for cheaper, faster, and more efficient means to print posters. If a poster is produced using lithography, it is most likely part of a limited edition. Over the years, photography has become the medium of choice for poster illustration. Reproductions of vintage posters, however, are commonplace and inexpensive, still beautiful for decorative purposes.

Original vintage posters can sell for high prices at auction and have created an entire submarket within the art trade. Art curators are interested in preserving these posters, which is not always an easy task. The first posters were backed with fabric, often being glued to linen to reinforce the printed paper. This method did not always age very well, and many of these posters have become brittle with age and have torn. Most high-quality posters today are still fabric backed, but improvements have been made in the process so that the material will remain in good shape for a much longer period than in the past. Adding fabric to the back of a poster not only helps strengthen and support the image, it also allows for easier restoration as well as preventing warping of the poster once framed. In restoring vintage posters, the curator's goal is to ensure that whatever work is done to the poster will not be damaging or irreversible in any way. Many things can damage the appearance of a poster including tape, stains, watermarks, and dirt. These can all be easily repaired, however, so that the poster can be restored to very close to its original appearance.

Extant vintage prints made using stone lithography are highly valuable. But rarity is difficult to determine because the number of prints made from a single design is unknown. Typical runs were from 250 to 3,000 posters and the posters actually pasted to buildings and billboards rarely survived. The posters that have survived until today are copies that were artists' own prints, collectors' prints, and leftovers found in printing warehouses. Vintage posters are rated by curators on a scale from A to D based on their condition, but even lower-rated posters, with a rating such as C or D, can still have significant value. Some of the most popular poster subjects for collectors are ocean liners, automobiles, and skiing.

JULES CHÉRET

1836–1932

Chéret began his career as an apprentice to a lithography company in Paris and moved to London for more training. When he returned to Paris he designed numerous advertising posters for theaters and cabarets, in particular the Folies Bergère. His favorite subjects were women. These women, rendered with some degree of modesty, were so popular that they were readily recognized throughout the city and the country as "the Chérettes." Moving to exploit the popularity of posters, Chéret introduced the *Maîtres de l'Affiche* poster series in 1895. The collection helped to define the poster as art, elevating it beyond the realm of advertising. The series included 256 lithographic plates of the original work of 97 artists. Chéret sent each subscriber a set of four prints on a monthly basis over a subscription period of five years. The vast majority of the posters in the series featured women, an early recognition that sex sells. One of Chéret's contemporaries and competitors in poster art was Henri de Toulouse-Lautrec, shown with Chéret at right (bottom) admiring one of Chéret's posters for the Moulin Rouge nightclub. At right (top) is a photograph of Chéret.

Promoting the American dancer Loïe Fuller who was performing at the Folies Bergère nightclub

JULES CHÉRET

Poster advertising the Palais de Glace, an ice-skating rink, on the Champs-Elysées in Paris

A "Chérette" turning up her lamp, fueled by the safe petrol, Saxoléine, 1896–1900

JULES CHÉRET

Poster for the Moulin Rouge nightclub, 1890

JULES CHÉRET

1894

ALFRED CHOUBRAC

1853–1902

Alfred Choubrac, a Parisian, studied art along with his brother and began the studio Workshops Choubrac, one of the first graphic design agencies in Paris. Choubrac specialized in the playbills of the Parisian nightclub scene, being commissioned by such venues as the Variety Theatre, Théâtre du Châtelet, Folies Bergères, Opera Comique, Moulin Rouge, Casino de Paris, Eldorado, and Cirque Fernando. He also executed a number of posters for bookstores. He produced over a 100 posters in his career. His talent extended to costume design as well.

Immediate left is yet another poster to celebrate the wonders of the dancer Loïe Fuller at the Folies Bergère; it is possible to see the fold lines of the poster, emphasizing such posters' original utilitarian purpose.

ALFRED CHOUBRAC

A poster to promote dances at Salle Wagram, a theater in Paris near the Arc de Triomphe, 1890

EUGÈNE GRASSET

1841–1917

Eugène Grasset was born in Lausanne, Switzerland. He is considered a pioneer in Art Nouveau design. After completing his education in Zurich where he studied architecture, he visited Egypt. His memories of that trip as well as his admiration of Japanese art both influenced his artistic expression, particularly obvious in many of his poster designs. Grasset first worked as a painter and sculptor in Lausanne. He moved to Paris in 1871, where he designed furniture, fabrics, and tapestries as well as ceramics and jewelry. In 1877 Grasset discovered graphic design, creating postcards and postage stamps for both France and Switzerland. Poster art quickly became his focus, however. He contributed works to Jules Chéret's *Maîtres de l'Affiche* poster series. In 1894 Grasset designed the poster at right to promote the second Salon des Cent, or Salon of the One Hundred, a commercial art exhibition in Paris that displayed and sold the works of 100 artists. Many of the well-known poster artists participated in the Salon—Grasset and Chéret were members—as well as designed posters to advertise it. Alphonse Mucha and Paul Émile Berthon created posters for later Salons.

EUGÈNE GRASSET

1894

EUGÈNE GRASSET

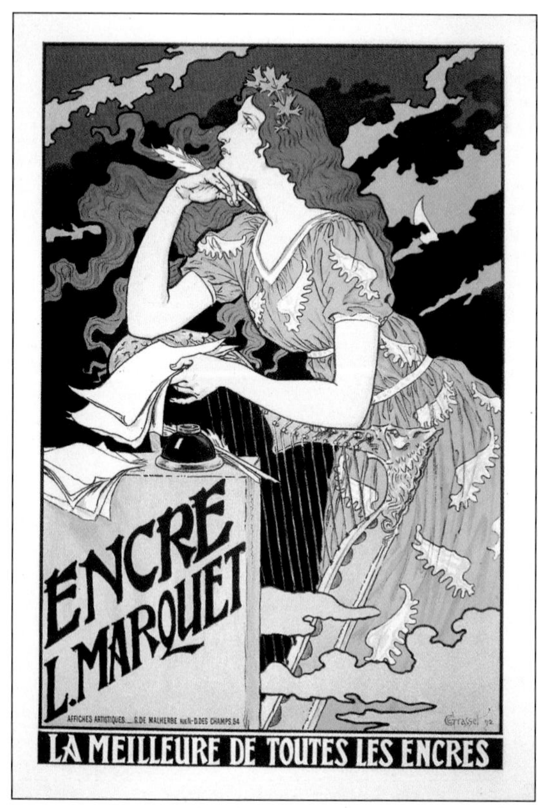

A poster to sell the ink of L. Marquet, 1892

EUGÈNE GRASSET

A poster for an exhibition of French decorative art at the Grafton Galleries in London, 1893

PAUL ÉMILE BERTHON

1872–1909

Queen Wilhelmina of the Netherlands, a portrait by Berthon once in the collection of the late actress Elizabeth Taylor

Paul Émile Berthon was a French artist who produced primarily posters and lithographs. He worked in the style of Art Nouveau, much like his contemporaries Mucha, Grasset, and Privat-Livemont. Berthon studied as a painter in Villefranche-sur-Mer, France, a village on the Mediterranean, before moving to Paris where he studied with Luc-Olivier Merson, a French academic painter and illustrator also known for his postage stamp and currency designs. The influence of Berthon's study of the decorative arts is obvious in his print making, which incorporates strong lines and natural details, such as flowers and vines.

PAUL ÉMILE BERTHON

PAUL ÉMILE BERTHON

A promotional poster for the
17th Salon des Cent in Paris, 1897

PAUL ÉMILE BERTHON

A cover for the illustrated literary magazine,
L'Ermitage, *1897*

HENRI DE TOULOUSE-LAUTREC

1864–1901

Henri Raymond de Toulouse-Lautrec-Monfa, referred to simply as Toulouse-Lautrec, worked in Paris in the late 19th century. Throughout his life he was plagued by an undefined congenital health problem, which many have attributed to a his aristocratic family's history of inbreeding. From a young age, Toulouse-Lautrec suffered from brittle bones that never fully healed after they broke, and as he aged, these malformed bones inhibited his natural growth and resulted in his unusually short stature. Although his torso was a normal adult size, his legs never grew longer than when he was 13 years old. Toulouse-Lautrec's physical handicaps effectively pushed him to pursue artistic studies because he was unable to participate in most other activities. Toulouse-Lautrec eventually found his niche in Montmarte, the bustling Bohemian neighborhood in Paris. Some of Toulouse-Lautrec's first subjects were the prostitutes of Montmarte, which would lead to his later, very famous paintings and posters of Paris' dance hall girls.

A cancan line composed of the dancers Eglantine, Cléopatre, Jane Avril, and Gazelle

Promoting the Moulin Rouge nightclub

HENRI DE TOULOUSE-LAUTREC

Promoting the Divan Japonais nightclub

Poster of Jane Avril, a well-known dancer in the Parisian cabarets

A poster advertising paper confetti, 1894; Toulouse-Lautrec's simple designs were inspired by Japanese woodblock prints

This poster promoted the novel Reine de Joie *by Victor Joze and proclaimed the novel could be found in local bookstores, 1892*

HENRI DE TOULOUSE-LAUTREC

Born in Ireland, May Belfort made a name for herself on the stages of Parisian nightclubs with her suggestive songs. One such musical double entendre was a song called "Daddy Wouldn't Buy Me a Bow Wow." She typically appeared on stage dressed in an English infant's frock and holding her ever-present black cat, as depicted by Toulouse-Lautrec in this 1895 promotional poster. Her lover, May Milton, was also a performer who likewise commissioned Toulouse-Lautrec's artistic genius in creating posters to promote her performances. Four separate lithographic stones and crachis, or spattered ink, were used to realize the finished composition in this poster of May Belfort.

HENRI DE TOULOUSE-LAUTREC

A photograph of Jane Avril

Extremely thin and given to jerky movements and sudden contortions, the Parisian dancer Jane Avril (1868-1943) was nicknamed La Mélinite, after an explosive. Her name at birth was Jeanne Beaudon, the daughter of a courtesan known as La Belle Elise and the Marchese Luigi de Font, an Italian aristocrat. When her mother committed her to the Pitié-Salpêtrière Hospital to be treated for "female hysterics," Jeanne put on a dancing exhibition that captivated everyone. Released from the hospital at the age of 16, she pursued a career in dancing by performing at the Parisian caberets. She adopted the stage name Jane Avril. First hired by the Moulin Rouge nightclub in 1889, within a few years she was headlining at the Jardin de Paris, one of the major café-concerts on the Champs-Élysées. In 1895, the owners of the Moulin Rouge offered her a great deal of money to take on the risky task of replacing Louise Weber, the most famous dancer in Paris. Jane met the challenge and became one of the most notable entertainers in the Parisian nightlife scene.

A poster commissioned by Jane Avril, 1899

FIRMIN BOUISSET

1859–1925

Bouisset is probably most famous for his posters for the French chocolate manufacturer Menier. Bouisset used his daughter Yvonne as a model to create what became an iconic image of a little girl using a piece of chocolate to write the company's name. Bouisset's work was part of Jules Chéret's *Maîtres de l'Affiche* poster series. The poster at right was created in 1893.

ÉMILE BERTRAND

1842–1912

Poster for Jules Massenet's production of Cendrillon (Cinderella), *advertising the première performance at the Théâtre National de l'Opéra-Comique in Paris, 1899.*

ALPHONSE MUCHA

1860–1939

Alphonse Mucha was born in what is now the Czech Republic. Being artistic from a young age, he moved to Paris after studying in Munich. To support himself, he worked for a printing company. One day in 1894, he was in the right place at the right time when he was the only artist in the office and was tasked with creating a poster for Sarah Bernhardt, the most famous actress in Europe at the time. Mucha's poster (near right) depicts an image of Bernhardt in the role of Gismonda. Bernhardt was so impressed by Mucha's work and the success his work brought her that she offered him a long-term contract. Mucha's posters of Bernhardt led to his great fame, and his unique artistic style triggered the Art Nouveau movement. In addition to the Bernhardt posters, Mucha began to receive a flood of other commissions, ranging from magazine ads to menus, postcards, and calendars.

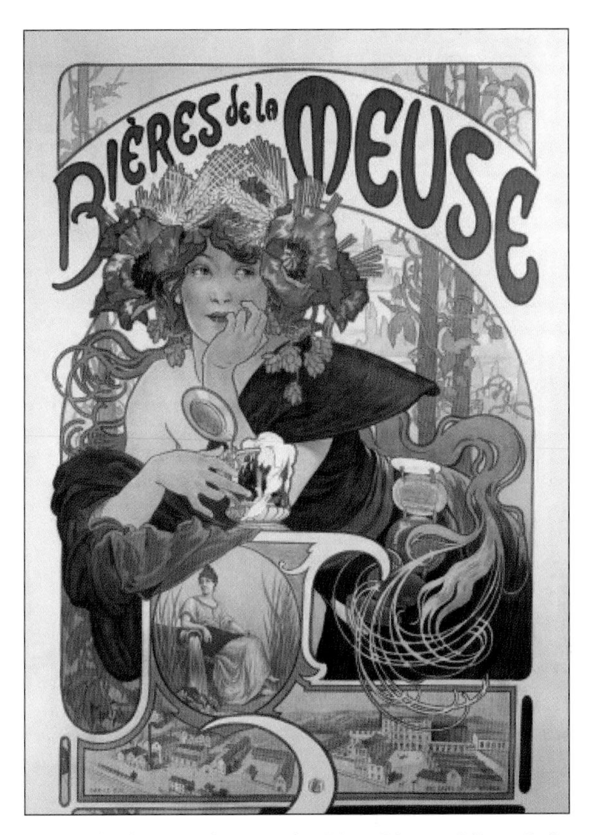

Poster for beer made near the River Meuse, Bières de la Meuse, 1897; the view of the brewery at the bottom of the poster was drawn by another artist.

A 1901 advertisement for Heidsieck & Co.
Monopole champagne

Alphonse Mucha created the logo LU for the biscuit (or cookie) company Biscuits Lefèvre-Utile

HENRI PRIVAT-LIVEMONT

1861–1936

Henri Privat-Livemont was born in Brussels, Belgium. He is best known for his Art Nouveau posters. From 1883 to 1889, he worked and studied in the studios of Lemaire, Lavastre & Duvignaud in Paris. He, with Lemaire, created the decor of the Theatre Francais as well as the Hôtel de Ville in Paris. He later returned to his hometown of Brussels, where he continued his decorative artistry. His works were included in Jules Chéret's *Maîtres de l'Affiche* poster series.

HENRI PRIVAT-LIVEMONT

The Green Fairie, Absinthe Robette, 1896

Advertising the chocolate biscuits (cookies) of a Belgian company, 1896

HENRI PRIVAT-LIVEMONT

1896

THÉOPHILE STEINLEN

1859–1923

Théophile Alexandre Steinlen, known simply as Steinlen, was a Swiss-born Art Nouveau painter and printmaker. He was born in Lausanne, where he attended university. He began work as a textile designer in Lausanne, but soon moved to the Montmartre section of Paris to pursue a career in art. In Paris, Steinlen met Adolphe Willette, another painter, who brought Steinlen to the Le Chat Noir cabaret. There, Steinlen meet the nightclub's owner who eventually commissioned him to create poster art for the club. Steinlen's work was shown at Paris' Les Salon des Indépendants—an exhibition established in 1884 in response to the rigid traditionalism of the official government-sponsored Salon—indicating his success in the Parisian art world. Much of his work was of cats, of which he was quite fond.

THÉOPHILE STEINLEN

An advertisement by Steinlen published in Chéret's Maîtres de l'Affiche *poster series, 1899*

THÉOPHILE STEINLEN

A poster advertising a tour of
Le Chat Noir's cabaret troup, 1896

Announcing an exhibition of many of the artists of the day, including Mucha, Steinlen, and de Feure; "Cocorico!" is the French equivalent of "Cock-a-doodle-do!"

SUZANNE FERRAND

French WWI posters, c. 1918, from a group of posters designed by school children and others:

"Keep wine for our soldiers."

"Grow wheat. It is gold for France."

HENRI DANGON

Not much is known about Henri Dangon except that he was an artist who was mobilized as part of the French army during World War I. In 1916, the Ministry of Beaux-Arts and the Ministry of War promised artists serving in the war that their work would be shown in official war exhibitions on the homefront. The government sponsored the Salon des Armées to show the work of the mobilized artists. The exhibition was very popular and realized 60,000 francs in proceeds, which supported not only needy artists at home but also the disabled. This poster by Dangon won first prize. A soldier holding a small wooden statue of winged victory that he has been carving.

RENÉ VINCENT

1879–1936

RENÉ VINCENT

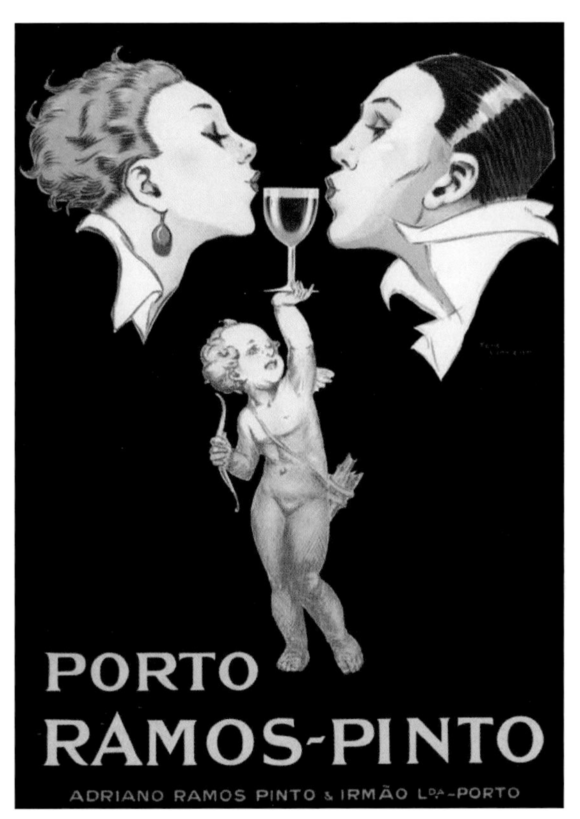

c. 1925

ROGER DE VALERIO

1886–1951

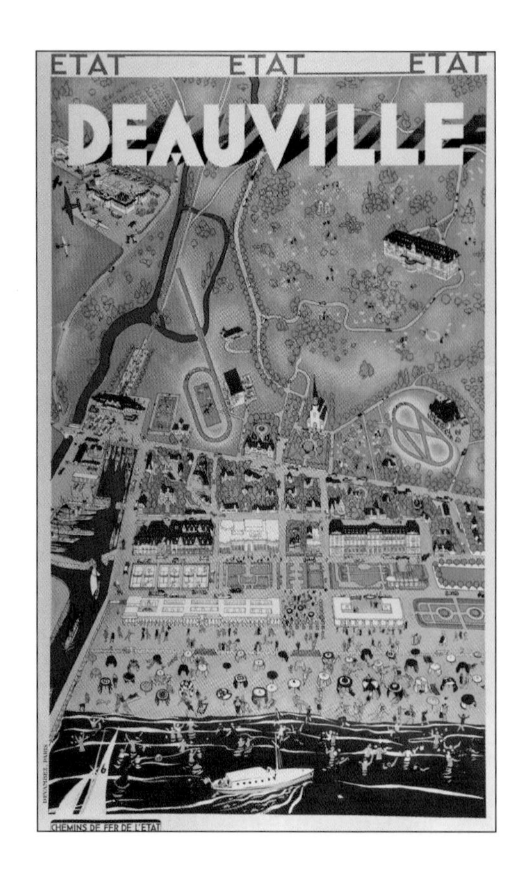

ROGER DE VALERIO

1936

ROGER DE VALERIO

1926

ROGER DE VALERIO

1928

ACHILLE MAUZAN

1883–1952

Mauzan was born on the French Riviera, but moved to Italy in 1905. In addition to being a decorative illustrator in the Art Deco style, he also painted and sculpted.

ACHILLE MAUZAN

c. 1920

ACHILLE MAUZAN

1936

ACHILLE MAUZAN

1922

LEONETTO CAPPIELLO

1875–1942

Leonetto Cappiello, who had no formal art training, was born in Livorno, Italy, and died in Cannes, France. He worked and lived most of his life in Paris. He was the first poster artist to use bold figures popping out of black backgrounds. He began his career as a caricaturist for numerous French periodicals. In 1902, a 24-page book of his caricatures was published entitled *Gens du Monde (People of High Society)*. At the turn of the century, however, his interest turned to poster art. His first poster was for the newspaper *Le Frou-Frou* in 1899. Cappiello's career as a poster artist began in earnest in 1900 when he contracted with the printer Pierre Vercasson, who wanted the posters he produced to stand out from the rest that were posted throughout the streets of Paris in order to attract lucrative new advertisers to his agency. After World War I, Cappiello joined a new agency, Devambez, with whom he remained until 1936. Devambez's clients stretched across Europe, introducing Cappiello and his work to a broader audience.

LEONETTO CAPPIELLO

LEONETTO CAPPIELLO

1899

LEONETTO CAPPIELLO

1922

LEONETTO CAPPIELLO

LEONETTO CAPPIELLO

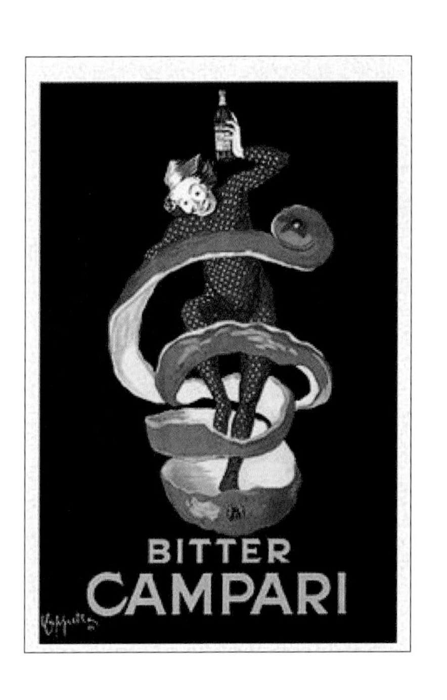

SANDY HOOK (GEORGE TABOUREAU)

1879-1960

SANDY HOOK (GEORGE TABOUREAU)

1920

MARCELLO DUDOVICH

1878–1962

Marcello Dudovich was not French but his poster art is readily recognizable to all who admire vintage posters. Dudovich was born in Trieste, Italy, and remained in Italy during his career.

A poster boasting of the seaside pleasures of Rimini, Italy, 1922

MARCELLO DUDOVICH

1946

MARCELLO DUDOVICH

MARCELLO DUDOVICH

1930

LEON BENIGNI

1892–1948

1929

EMIL CARDINAUX

1877–1936

A Swiss artist promoting the summer in his homeland, 1921

GUILLAUME ROGER

1867-1943

An encouragment to head to the south of France to the Côte d'Azur (or French Riviera), 1926

EDOUARD COURCHINOUX

1891-1968

An encouragment to head to the north of France to the village of Le Touquet-Paris-Plage near Calais, 1926

JULIEN LACAZE

1886–1971

JULIEN LACAZE

HENRY LE MONNIER

1893-1978

1926

CHARLES LOUPOT

1892-1962

1929

PAUL COLIN

1892–1985

Paul Colin, a student of Eugène Vallin and Victor Prouvé, was made famous in 1925 by his poster for La Revue Nègre, which helped launch the career of the American singer Josephine Baker, who later became his mistress. Colin worked for over 40 years in the theater, creating not only posters but also sets and costumes. His first leanings were to the Art Deco style, but he quickly moved on to develop a highly personal style that is difficult to categorize.

At left, Paul Colin's interpretation of the magnificent and mysterious dancer Loïe Fuller

PAUL COLIN

Josephine Baker as Paul Colin drew her (above) in his famous poster promoting La Revue Nègre, *1925*

Josephine Baker (below) bowled over the Parisians with her sensual and uninhibited dance routines in La Revue Nègre.

ADOLPHE MOURON (CASSANDRE)

1901–1968

Adolphe Jean-Marie Mouron, known simply as Cassandre, is credited with developing innovative graphic-design solutions in advertising. He worked in Paris between the First and Second World Wars. Cassandre was born in Ukraine, but moved to Paris in the 1920s, thriving in the city's creative and artistic environment. After studying at the Ecole des Beaux-Arts and the Académie Julian, and influenced by Cubist and Surrealist imagery, he began to incorporate that imagery into his designs in poster making. By the mid-1930s, he was being commissioned to design magazine covers by such periodicals as *Harper's Bazaar*. He was also an innovator in designing typeface. Cassandre developed Bifur in 1929, the sans serif Acier Noir in 1935, and in 1937 an all-purpose font called Peignot. In 1936, his works were exhibited at the Museum of Modern Art in New York City. Today he is best known for his travel posters. The enormous, hulking prow of the *Normandie* trans-Atlantic ocean liner (at right) on a poster created by Cassandre is one of the most famous and iconic in the history of poster designs.

ADOLPHE MOURON (CASSANDRE)

ADOLPHE MOURON (CASSANDRE)

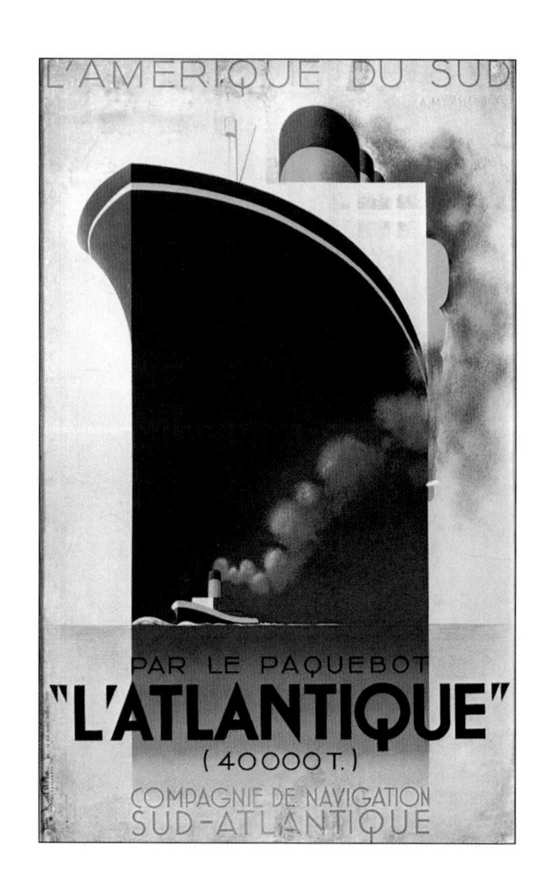

ADOLPHE MOURON (CASSANDRE)

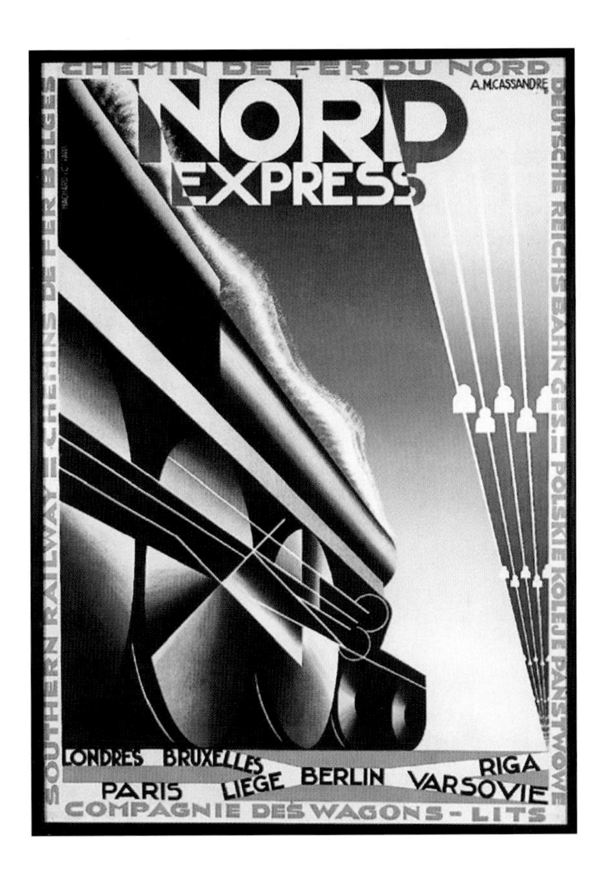

JEAN CARLU

1900–1997

Jean Carlu was a French graphic designer who specialized in posters. In the early 1920s he worked for an agency that created advertising campaigns. It was during these years that he adopted the Art Deco style for his poster designs. His fame rests mainly on two posters: one for Monsavon, a soap company, and another for the Théâtre Pigalle. He also designed a label for the 1924 vintage of Château Mouton-Rothschild (top). During World War II, the U.S. government hired Carlu, who had moved to the U.S., to create ads that would encourage Americans to work hard and increase production as a form of patriotism.

JEAN CARLU

For the Parisian department store Le Bon Marché

JEAN CARLU

For Théâtre Pigalle

JEAN CARLU

For the soap company Monsavon

INDEX

Manuel Robbe

René Vincent, 1914